UNOFFICIAL GUIDES

MINECRAFT:
Virtual Reality

CHERRY LAKE PUBLISHING • ANN ARBOR, MICHIGAN

by Josh Gregory

Published in the United States of America by Cherry Lake Publishing
Ann Arbor, Michigan
www.cherrylakepublishing.com

Reading Adviser: Marla Conn, Read With Me Now
Photo Credits: Cover and pages 6 and 11, ©Tinxi/Shutterstock; page 8, ©Ken Ishii/Stringer/Getty Images; page 9, ©IhorStudio/Shutterstock; page 10, ©PR Image Factory/Shutterstock; page 12, ©Tom Cooper/Stringer/Getty Images; page 15, ©Gavrylovaphoto/Shutterstock; page 16, ©catwalker/Shutterstock; page 17, ©bearinmind/Shutterstock; page 18, ©Phil's Mommy/Shutterstock; page 19, ©v74/Shutterstock; page 20, ©izusek/Getty Images; page 21, ©Dusan Petkovic/Shutterstock; page 24, ©LightField Studios/Shutterstock; page 25, ©Inti St Clair/Getty Images; page 26, ©mihailomilovanovic/Getty Images; all other images by Josh Gregory

Library of Congress Cataloging-in-Publication Data has been filed and is available at catalog.loc.gov

Cherry Lake Publishing would like to acknowledge the work of the Partnership for 21st Century Learning. Please visit www.p21.org for more information.

Printed in the United States of America
Corporate Graphics

Contents

Chapter 1

A New Way to Explore

f you've ever played *Minecraft*, you know how fun it can be to explore the game's huge worlds. There are lush, green forests and sprawling, sandy deserts. You can climb to the top of a snowy mountain

There is always another hill to climb or underground cave to explore in *Minecraft*.

You can build your own houses, castles, and other places to explore in *Minecraft*.

peak or tunnel through an underground cave system. Along the way, you might befriend a variety of wild animals or do battle with dangerous enemies. And because no two *Minecraft* adventures are the same, there is always something new to see or do when you start a new game.

Of course, *Minecraft*'s most exciting feature is that it gives you the ability to reshape the world however you like. You can build a tower that reaches high into the sky, or you can tunnel deep under the surface. You can build any kind of building or landform you can imagine, from a massive castle to a mountaintop lair.

Traveling through a world you've built by yourself can be a lot of fun. Today, there is a way to explore your *Minecraft* creations in even greater detail. Thanks to the power of virtual reality (VR) technology, you can get up close and personal with the world of *Minecraft*.

Instead of looking at the game on a screen, you wear a **headset** that puts the virtual world right in front of your eyes. It takes up all of your vision. There

A VR headset can completely change the way you see the world of *Minecraft*.

A Virtual Living Room

Playing an **immersive** video game like *Minecraft* in VR can be a surprisingly tiring experience. Luckily, the game comes with a built-in feature that lets users take a break from the full VR experience without stopping their game or even removing the VR headset.

With just one button press, VR *Minecraft* players can switch to a view called the virtual living room. Instead of feeling like they are in the world of *Minecraft*, players will see a comfy living room all around them. The living room has a big TV with *Minecraft* on the screen, so the game can continue even while players relax!

are no distractions from the real world. It is like you are really there. If you want to look in a different direction, all you need to do is move your head. Everything you look at seems life-sized. It is not a flat image. When a creeper or some other mob comes running at you, it really looks like it's getting closer! When you climb to the top of a tower and look off the edge, it really feels like you're high above the ground.

VR headsets are some of today's hottest tech devices. They can be used for everything from playing video games to watching movies. Have you ever wanted to see the Grand Canyon or the Great Wall of China? VR lets you travel to exciting locations around the world without leaving the house. With all VR has to offer, it's no wonder that it has become so popular.

There have been many updates and changes to *Minecraft* since it was first released in 2009. From multiplayer mode to enemy mobs, each one of these updates has made the game even more fun and interesting to play. Virtual reality could end up being one of the biggest, most incredible additions in

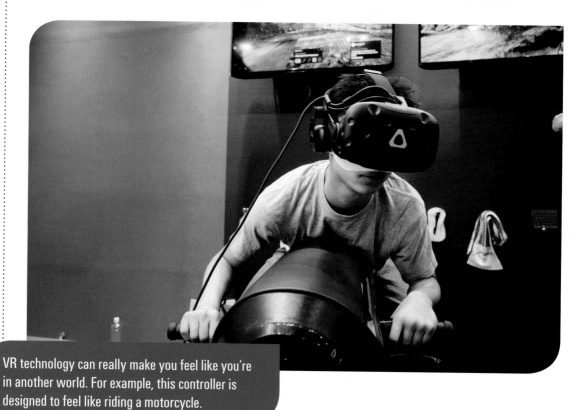

VR technology can really make you feel like you're in another world. For example, this controller is designed to feel like riding a motorcycle.

When you first start using VR, you'll probably try to reach out to touch things that aren't really there!

Minecraft history. After all, it combines an exciting area of technology with one of the most popular video games ever made. What could be more exciting than that?

Are you curious about virtual reality? Whether you've tried it before or you're only just hearing about it for the first time, there is a lot to learn about this amazing technology. But before you know it, you'll be exploring the virtual world of *Minecraft* and your other favorite games as if you'd been doing it your whole life.

Chapter 2

Virtual Worlds

Virtual reality is one of today's most talked about forms of cutting-edge technology. But believe it or not, the basic ideas behind VR are not new at all. Scientists and **engineers** have been researching the possibilities of virtual reality for decades. In fact, the idea for a wearable device that puts video screens right in front of users' eyes was first dreamed up way

Today, many developers are working to create new ways of using VR technology.

Modern VR headsets are lightweight and much easier to use than earlier VR technology.

back in the 1960s. This idea wasn't all that different from the VR headsets we use today!

VR technology has improved a great deal over time. One reason for this is that computers have become more powerful. They are able to create realistic graphics that fool your brain into thinking they are real. Another reason for VR's improvement is that engineers have built better **hardware**. The earliest VR headsets were heavy and uncomfortable. Some even weighed so much that a user's head could not support

A NASA test pilot tries out a VR simulation of a high-speed airplane.

the weight. Instead, the headsets were mounted to the ceiling.

In the 1970s and 1980s, VR became a popular way for the military to train pilots. Instead of jumping into the cockpit of a dangerous, expensive airplane, student pilots could use VR equipment to go through realistic training lessons. The National Aeronautics and Space Administration (NASA) used similar technology to train astronauts. As a result, military

Minecraft isn't the only best-selling video game to take the VR world by storm. In fact, video games are one of the most popular uses of VR technology today. Some, like *Minecraft*, are VR versions of games that were already enjoyed by millions of players. Others are brand-new experiences built from the ground up to take advantage of VR features.

Because VR technology has only recently become popular for home use, many of the games available today are still fairly simple. However, developers are already hard at work on more detailed and immersive experiences.

and NASA scientists and engineers worked hard to improve VR technology. Their work has helped lead to the VR headsets we have today.

Today's virtual reality technology is more powerful, lightweight, and easier to use than ever before. It also costs a lot less than the experimental VR tech of the past. This means more people have a chance to try it out for themselves. What was once the kind of technology that only appeared in science-fiction movies is now a common household device for many people.

All modern VR technology is based on a combination of hardware and **software**. VR hardware includes headsets, game controllers, and sensors. It also includes the computers, smartphones, and consoles used to run games and other VR content. Software consists of the different games, videos, and other programs you need for a VR experience.

Some VR systems are more complex than others. For basic VR experiences, all you need is a smartphone and a cardboard headset to hold the phone in front of your eyes. With this kind of setup, you can move your head to look around a virtual world. However, your other movements don't have any effect on anything that happens on-screen.

A more advanced VR system might require a high-end computer, a variety of handheld motion controllers, a powerful VR headset, and an empty room with sensors placed around the edges. With this kind of VR system, you can walk around in the virtual world. Your head movements and body movements are tracked separately. This means you could walk backward while turning your head, or crouch down to look more closely at something on the ground. You can even move your arms around to pick up objects in the virtual world.

Most of today's VR setups, including the ones used for *Minecraft*, fall somewhere between the most basic and high-end systems. However, inventors are always looking for ways to make VR technology better. Soon enough, powerful VR systems might be as common in people's homes as television screens or laptops are.

Chapter 3

Getting Started

Are you ready to jump into the world of VR *Minecraft*? You'll need a few things before you can get started on your adventure. First, you need to decide which system you will use to play the game. While *Minecraft* is available on many different game systems and other devices, the VR features only work on the Windows 10 PC version and the Samsung

If you already have a Samsung Galaxy phone, the Gear VR headset is the easiest, cheapest way to play *Minecraft* in VR.

Ask a parent if you need help downloading the *Minecraft* app to your phone.

Gear VR mobile version. This means tablets, iPhones, and game consoles cannot be used to play in VR.

Second, if you are going to play the Samsung Gear VR version, you will need a fairly new Samsung Galaxy smartphone. You will also need the Gear VR headset and a **compatible** game controller. Finally, you'll need to download the correct version of the game from the Oculus Store. If you already have the right kind of phone, this is the cheapest and simplest way to start playing *Minecraft* in VR.

The Windows 10 version requires more equipment. First, you'll need a fast, up-to-date PC with the latest version of Windows installed. Second, you'll need a VR headset that is compatible with the game. The two that are officially supported by the *Minecraft* creators are the Oculus Rift and Microsoft's Windows Mixed Reality system. Either one will give you roughly the same experience with *Minecraft*. It all comes down to which one you find more comfortable.

If you use a laptop or desktop computer to play *Minecraft*, make sure it is fast enough to support a VR headset.

The Xbox One controller will work with both the Windows 10 and Gear VR versions of *Minecraft*.

Just like the Gear VR version, you will need a game controller to play the Windows 10 version of *Minecraft* in VR. You can use a mouse and keyboard, just like you would to play the game without a VR headset. However, it can be hard to play this way in VR because you can't see your hands. You might prefer to use a standard video game controller instead. One good option is Microsoft's Xbox One controller. If you have an Xbox, you probably already have at least one of these controllers at home.

If you think it sounds like you'll need a lot of fancy tech equipment to play *Minecraft* in VR, you're right! While VR technology is simpler and less expensive than ever, it is still not cheap. Putting together a VR system at home can cost hundreds or even thousands of dollars. If you don't already have some of this equipment at home, you might not want to run out and buy it all.

Many schools purchase VR equipment for students to use.

Many stores give shoppers the chance to try VR systems before buying them.

Luckily, there is probably a way for you to try VR *Minecraft* or other VR experiences even if you don't have your own equipment. Many technology stores and video game stores have demo units available for customers to try. Another option might be to ask a teacher or librarian at your school about VR. Some schools have equipment for students to use.

However you decide to play the game, the experience is roughly the same. Simply start up the game like you would when playing it regularly. If you already have a saved game, you can even jump right into the world you've started. Otherwise, you can start exploring and building from scratch.

When you first start playing in VR, you might want to spend some time in the game's Options menus. Here, you'll find a variety of adjustments that can make the game more comfortable to play or easier to control. For example, you can adjust the way movement works in VR. Some people like to control the game the same way they do when playing normally. They simply press the control stick or keyboard in the direction they want to walk.

However, for other players, these movement controls can be disorienting when combined with head movement. For this reason, the **default** setting in VR *Minecraft* changes the controls a little. When you press on the control stick or keyboard to turn your character, you will not turn smoothly. Instead, you will turn in large segments at once. You will also hear a quiet sound effect each time you turn. This default setting allows you to turn your head for smooth, smaller movements and use the controller to make bigger moves. If you don't like it, feel free to turn it off!

You can also adjust how the game's heads-up display (HUD) shows up on-screen. The HUD is the

While *Minecraft*'s official VR mode is limited to the Oculus Rift, Samsung Gear VR, and Windows Mixed Reality systems, some players have found ways to bring the experience to other systems. They have programmed their own **mods** and **hacks** to get the game working on the HTC Vive and PlayStation VR headsets. They have even found ways to make the game work with motion controls, so players can mine and swing weapons by moving their arms around. While all these features can be very cool, they are not officially supported by *Minecraft*'s creators. They can be difficult to install, and they don't always work correctly.

It is no surprise that players have found creative new ways to use *Minecraft* in VR. Fans have been building mods and hacks for the game since it was first released in 2009. This is part of what made the game so popular in the first place!

information about your character's health, hunger, and **inventory** that is displayed on the screen as you play. It also includes the various text messages the game displays on the screen. The default setting allows the HUD to "float" on top of the game world as you move your head around. However, you can change it to stay locked to the same area of your vision at all times.

Everyone has different opinions on which settings are best for enjoying *Minecraft* in VR. Feel free to play around with the menus until you get it just right.

Chapter 4

Tips and Advice

Virtual reality can be a lot of fun. It offers an experience that is different from anything else. It is changing the way people play video games, watch movies, and more. However, using VR equipment is a lot more complicated than simply turning on a TV, computer, or game console. There are

It can take a little bit of work to get your VR equipment up and running correctly.

It is best to avoid standing up or walking around while playing *Minecraft* in VR.

a lot of things you have to keep in mind if you want to have a good time while playing *Minecraft* and other games in VR.

Remember, it is always important to consider your safety while playing VR. Some types of VR allow players to stand up or wander around a room as they play. These VR systems include visual hints to show players when they are getting too close to walls or other objects. However, *Minecraft* does not work this way in VR. It is meant to be played while sitting still.

To avoid falling down or crashing into things, stay seated in a comfortable chair or couch while you play. If you need to get up or walk around, take the headset off.

In addition to sitting still, make sure there is nothing around you that you can knock over and break as you're playing. You won't be able to see anything in your real-world surroundings. If you get excited and move too quickly, you could easily hit nearby objects or people without noticing.

Ask for help adjusting your VR headset if it isn't comfortable or the picture isn't clear.

You might have a hard time hearing things around you if you have the game's volume too high in your headphones. Try to find a volume level that lets you enjoy the game's immersive sound while also letting you hear people talking to you. If a parent or someone else needs to get your attention while you're adventuring in VR, they shouldn't have to yell.

It's also important to make sure you are comfortable before you start playing. VR headsets can be heavy. You want it to sit just right on your head and face. Spend some time making adjustments to the various straps and sliding parts on your headset. Make sure the VR image is displaying clearly in front of your eyes. Adjusting the headset can give you a clearer, more focused view.

Not everyone reacts the same way when they try VR for the first time. Some people have no problem jumping in and enjoying themselves. But others have issues with motion sickness. Some people start feeling sick to their stomachs almost as soon as they strap on a VR headset. Others can only play for a short time. If you start feeling ill, take a break right away. You might eventually get more used to VR and be able to play longer. Do not try to force yourself, though. If you get motion sickness easily, you can also try adjusting some of the settings in the game's Options menu. Sometimes all it takes is a few small tweaks to make the game more comfortable to play.

Playing a game like *Minecraft* in VR can be an incredibly absorbing experience. It is unlike anything you've ever done before in a video game. However, it is important not to get too lost in the game world. Take

What will you do next as you explore the world of *Minecraft* in virtual reality?

For the most part, playing *Minecraft* in VR is exactly the same as playing it the regular way. All of the tricks and techniques you've learned will work just as well in VR as they do in other versions of the game. You can still build things, fight monsters, and seek out valuable treasure.

You can even join up with friends for online VR multiplayer. Your *Minecraft* characters can come face-to-face with each other. It's almost like hanging out with them in real life! Show off your gear, duel in a friendly battle, or simply hang out in a custom-built castle. As with anything in *Minecraft*, how you want to play is all up to you.

breaks regularly, even if you're having fun. It is always a good idea to give your eyes a break from the stress of staring at the screens in your VR headset. It is also a good idea to stand up, stretch, and move around. Sitting too long can cause a number of health issues!

The most important thing to remember as you play is to always have fun. Get out there and start exploring the world of *Minecraft* for yourself. You never know what you will find around the next corner!

Glossary

compatible (kuhm-PAT-uh-buhl) able to be used together

default (di-FAWLT) standard; in effect unless you choose something else

engineers (en-juh-NEERS) people trained to design and build things

hacks (HAKS) homemade, unofficial modifications to computer programs or objects

hardware (HAHRD-wair) computer equipment

headset (HED-set) a wearable device that places screens directly in front of the user's eyes to create the experience of virtual reality

immersive (i-MUR-siv) able to make users feel totally absorbed in an experience

inventory (IN-vuhn-tor-ee) a display of the items your character is carrying in *Minecraft*

mods (MAHDS) user-created modifications to a video game

software (SAWFT-wair) computer programs

Find Out More

BOOKS

Gregory, Josh. *Virtual Reality*. Ann Arbor, MI: Cherry Lake Publishing, 2018.

Milton, Stephanie. *Minecraft Essential Handbook*. New York: Scholastic, 2015.

Milton, Stephanie. *Minecraft: Guide to Exploration*. New York: Del Rey, 2017.

WEBSITES

Minecraft
https://minecraft.net/en
At this official *Minecraft* website, you can learn more about the game or download a copy of the PC version.

Minecraft Wiki
https://minecraft.gamepedia.com/Minecraft_Wiki
Minecraft's many fans work together to maintain this detailed guide to the game.

Index

About the Author

Josh Gregory is the author of more than 125 books for kids. He has written about everything from animals to technology to history. A graduate of the University of Missouri–Columbia, he currently lives in Chicago, Illinois.